COPING WITH
SEXUAL
HARASSMENT

1V Thurston

Published in 2018 by The Rosen Publishing Group, Inc.
29 East 21st Street, New York, NY 10010

Copyright © 2018 by The Rosen Publishing Group, Inc.

First Edition

Library of Congress Cataloging-in-Publication Data

Names: Thurston, IV, author.
Title: Coping with sexual harassment / IV Thurston.
Description: New York, NY: Rosen Publishing, 2018. | Series: Coping | Includes bibliographical references and index. | Audience: Grades 7–12.
Identifiers: ISBN 9781508176954 (library bound) | ISBN 9781508178538 (paperback)
Subjects: LCSH: Sexual harassment—Juvenile literature. | Sexual abuse victims—Juvenile literature.
Classification: LCC HQ1237.T48 2018 | DDC 305.3—dc23

Manufactured in China

CONTENTS

Introduction 4

CHAPTER ONE
What Is Sexual Harassment? 8

CHAPTER TWO
If You're a Victim of Sexual Harassment 25

CHAPTER THREE
How to Help Yourself 43

CHAPTER FOUR
Technology and Harassment 60

CHAPTER FIVE
How to Be an Ally 78

GLOSSARY 95
FOR MORE INFORMATION 97
FOR FURTHER READING 102
BIBLIOGRAPHY 104
INDEX 108

INTRODUCTION

Sexual harassment can happen anywhere—at school, work, or when you are having fun—and at any time. Learn what to look for.

Today is the day. You've been planning a day out with your friends for weeks. Standing in front of the mirror, getting ready, you think about how you wouldn't have been allowed to go out with your friends without a chaperone even just a year ago. You and your friends have been waiting to see this movie since you streamed the trailer. This is growing up. You brush your hair for the millionth time and decide you are ready.

Finally, you see the car turn the corner and you are already on the street before the car stops. The car is filled with all of your best friends. You've known them since you were in elementary school, when you were a little kid. You laugh and scream and sing on the way to the theater.

After the movie, the real fun begins—going to get some food! Going out with your friends to get some food is the best. No parents. You can order whatever you want. And you can talk about the movie.

As you walk over to the mall, a car drives by and slows down. You look over. The window is open. An older man, about your dad's age, sticks his head out the window and yells at you and your friends: "Hey! You girls are sexy!!! Want a ride?"

He drives off.

One of your friends asks, "What did he say?!?"

"I can't repeat it," you reply.

"What a perv!" another shouts.

Finally, at the food court with your friends, the french fries don't taste as good. No one is laughing anymore. You know they are just words, but they hurt. And he was so much older than you. Why would anyone say that? You don't know how to feel anymore, but you do know that your day out has been ruined.

What do you do? Whom do you tell? Your parents? What can they even do about it?

Your parents pick up you and your friends. You are not the same excited group that went out earlier.

You dad asks, "Something happen? You are awfully quiet."

Your best friend, who always has the quickest answers, says, "The movie was just disappointing, you know?"

These teenagers have been sexually harassed. Sadly, they are not alone. According to Stop Street Harassment, in the United States alone, 65 percent of women have experienced sexual harassment on the street—and that percentage is even higher in some countries! Clearly, sexual harassment is a major problem in societies all around the world. This resource will help you understand not only what sexual harassment is, but also what to do about it if it happens to you or someone you know.

CHAPTER ONE

What Is Sexual Harassment?

egally, sexual harassment is defined as unwelcome sexual advances, requests for sexual favors, and other verbal or physical actions of a sexual nature. Although not recognized in federal courts until the 1970s, the last forty years or so have seen great gains in our legal understanding of sexual harassment. There are still many areas that need improvement, however, and the sexual harassment of teens is especially a place that needs to have stronger laws and more safeguards.

Unwelcome

The key word in the aforementioned definition is "unwelcome." You are allowed to do anything you want within the law with someone if both parties consent. Courts have generally concluded that a victim of sexual harassment does not have to show that he or she was not interested for harassment to occur. To think of it another way, assume that people do not want to talk to you, touch you, or

The words "stop" and "no" are your best allies when you need to make yourself clear. If someone is making you uncomfortable, do not be afraid to speak up.

do anything else in a sexual manner. That is normal. What is not normal is harassment. It is important to remember, at all times, that every victim of sexual harassment is exactly that: a victim.

If you have experienced unwelcome advances, do not be afraid to speak out. You have been wronged and did nothing to invite the other person's behavior, comments, or actions. Also, do not be afraid to speak out if you witness someone being sexually harassed. Ignoring harassment is not a useful strategy. Harassers rarely voluntarily stop harassing people.

In the introduction, a group of friends had their day ruined by the man in the car. That was sexual harassment. Sexual harassment is when someone makes you feel uncomfortable or upset because he or she did something unwanted to you and it included sexual overtones. Sexual harassment is also a form of bullying. Like all bullying it is designed to hurt someone or make him or her afraid. Not only is the definition of sexual harassment broad, it can manifest itself in many ways. Here is a partial list of actions that definitely qualify as sexual harassment:

- Making sexual gestures
- Talking about someone in a lewd manner
- Making sexualized "jokes"
- Repeatedly asking someone out even after the person has said no

- Spreading rumors of a sexual nature—this can be done person to person, via text, or on social media
- Purposefully rubbing up against someone to touch his or her body
- Writing or drawing sexual graffiti about someone in a public place
- Touching, grabbing, or pinching someone in a sexual way or in his or her genital area(s)
- Sharing pornography with someone
- Saying sexualized things about someone or making offers to someone using a fake name or anonymously online
- Requesting "nudes" (naked photographs) or sending naked pictures of themselves
- Sending sexual messages of any form or posting sexual content on someone else's social media page(s)

It is important to know that sexual harassment is not the same as sexual assault. While sexual harassment is not to be tolerated, sexual assault is someone physically acting on his or her desires when the other person does not want it. Sexual assault can be something as small as an unwanted kiss and as horrible as forced sexual intercourse or rape. Whether it is sexual harassment or assault, remember that it is never your fault that these things happened!

Clarence Thomas versus Anita Hill

Supreme Court Justice Clarence Thomas was all set to be approved to be confirmed by the US Senate when Anita Hill's complaints against him became public. The firestorm created by Hill's accusations made Thomas's confirmation hearings must-watch television, with more than ten million viewers tuning in. It also greatly increased the public's awareness of sexual harassment, turning it into a national conversation.

For many, it was a he-said, she-said situation—neither side had 100 percent proof. Anita Hill claimed that while she was working with Clarence Thomas he talked about the size of his penis and his abilities to pleasure a woman. She was afraid to speak up at the time because she was afraid of losing her job.

Hill spoke before the Congressional committee and said, "I began to feel severe stress on the job. I began to be concerned that Clarence Thomas might take out his anger with me by degrading me or not giving me important assignments. I also thought that he might find an excuse for dismissing me."

(continued on the next page)

Anita Hill's testimony during the US Supreme Court nomination for Clarence Thomas made sexual harassment an everyday topic in America.

(continued from the previous page)

Thomas responded, "This is a circus. It's a national disgrace. It is a high-tech lynching for uppity blacks who in any way deign to think for themselves and it is a message that unless you kowtow to an old order you will be lynched, destroyed, caricatured by a committee of the US Senate rather than hung from a tree."

The Senate eventually confirmed Thomas 52–48, which is the closest Supreme Court confirmation vote in US history.

In 2010, Virginia Thomas, Clarence Thomas's wife, left a voicemail for Anita Hill asking her if she wanted to apologize. Hill responded, "The call was inappropriate." She added that she had "no intention of apologizing because I testified truthfully about my experience and I stand by that testimony."

But What About Flirting?

Flirting is a gray area. The easiest way to know if something is flirtation or harassment is to answer this question: Do both people want this to happen, or is it only one person? Here are some examples that may help you understand the crucial difference between flirting and harassment.

Flirting is simultaneously one of the most exciting and stressful parts about getting older. Just remember, flirting, too, has to be a two-way street.

- You and your boyfriend or girlfriend have been starting to get serious together. You joke about sending nudes to each other and then when asked if you would send one, you say, "No way!" Instead of him or her respecting your wishes, your partner continues to pressure you to do so. This is harassment.

15

- You wear a new outfit to school. A classmate tells you that it looks nice. That is not harassment. That is simply a compliment. If that person then tells you that it makes your bottom look sexy or that your clothes make him or her want to do sexual things to you, that is harassment.
- A classmate asks you out on a date. You are not attracted to him or her and don't want to hurt his or her feelings, so you tell the classmate that you are busy that day. He or she asks you out again. You make up another excuse. This sort of lying is common and is often done to avoid making the other person feel bad. However, sometimes people become more aggressive when they have not been firmly told no. When that happens, he or she might start sending you too many messages or even messages that refer to sex. He or she might even start showing up everywhere you are. That has moved from someone innocently asking you out and has crossed the line into sexual harassment.

As you get older and perhaps date more, you may find yourself in awkward, or uncomfortable, situations. This is part of dating—and life in general— and it simply cannot be avoided. The best way to avoid getting yourself into awkward situations is by being honest and up-front with people. In the short term, it might be easier to make up an excuse for why you cannot go out with someone. But it would have been better to respond to the request for a date with honesty and clarity. You can say something as simple as, "I am flattered that you are interested in me, but I don't have the same feelings for you. Sorry." Hopefully, the person will appreciate your tact and stop asking you out.

One final note on flirting: flirting is a part of life. It is also fun and exciting—it is nice to have someone pay attention to you and want to engage in witty conversation. While it is easy to get caught up in the moment and flirt, always keep this in mind: flirting between adults and teenagers is never okay. It is inappropriate, and the adult is always at fault. An adult should know better. Always tell someone if an adult has stopped acting friendly and has started to flirt with you. And remember, you did not do anything wrong.

Where Does Sexual Harassment Take Place?

Sadly, there is no safe space that can be guaranteed to be free from sexual harassment. There are certain places where it is more likely to occur, however, and equipping yourself with this knowledge can help you recognize and then act appropriately upon incidents of sexual harassment.

Sadly, school is the number one place where teens encounter sexual harassment. What is your school doing to help students?

The list that follows outlines some of the places where sexual harassment most often occurs:

- **School**: You spend more time at school than anywhere else. It is also a place that cannot be 100 percent supervised because the students greatly outnumber faculty and staff. According to an article for *U.S. News and World Report* by Allie Bidwell, the University of Illinois at Urbana-Champaign conducted a study of nearly 1,400 students. It found that 27 percent of girls and 25 percent of boys reported experiencing verbal or physical sexual harassment. In the same study, researchers were surprised at where sexual harassment was happening at schools. The majority of incidents occurred in hallways, closely followed by classrooms (22.7 percent and 21.4 percent respectively) with only 13 percent occurring inside school gyms and 9.7 percent taking place near lockers. The most common form of sexual harassment reported was unwanted physical touching, at 21.6 percent.
- **Religious spaces (churches, temples, mosques, etc.)**: This may seem counterintuitive. Religious spaces are the places where people go for spirituality and to be closer to a higher power. However, these are also spaces where people place a great deal of trust in others and become

vulnerable. Beyond physical touching and verbal abuse, some places of worship have reported church workers watching and showing pornography to their victims.

- **On the street**: Statistics vary, but catcalling is one of the most common forms of sexual harassment. Both men and women may be victims of catcalling, but like most victims of harassment in general, women greatly outnumber men. The group of teenagers in the introduction were victims of catcalling.

- **At work**: More and more teenagers are working than ever before, and over summer break, of course, the number of teenage employees swells. Sadly, the workplace is one of the most common places for the sexual harassment of teens to occur. Major corporations and employers of teens, including Burger King, McDonald's, and Starbucks, have had to pay money to victims of sexual harassment. Managers and coworkers alike have harassed people at work and have even gone so far as to send unwelcome and explicit text messages. Also, some sexual predators, knowing that many places hire teenagers to work during the summer, use these places as a kind of hunting ground where they know there will be ample victims.

- **Online and over the phone**: Between social media and apps like Kik, Twitter, Instagram,

Bullying and sexual harassment can follow teens home in a way that was unthinkable to previous generations. Social media is a growing concern as harassment can now take place anytime.

Tumblr, Vine, and Snapchat—just to name a few—teenagers today find it harder to leave their school day behind than any generation before them. On any of these platforms, and inside any of these apps, sexual harassment can occur. Sending unsolicited texts and nudes are extremely common practices. So is sharing nude photos without permission that someone may have sent to another person, such as a partner, in the past. Additionally, many teenagers have experienced having their sex lives used against them, which is often known as slut shaming.

Myths & FACTS

Myth: Sexual harassment is often exaggerated, and most so-called harassment is harmless flirtation.

Fact: This is a false and dangerous statement. Most harassment has nothing to do with flirtation or true, sincere social or sexual interest. Like bullying, harassment is designed to intimidate and frighten. It can also be insulting or simply offensive to hear someone speak about your body that way. Many victims of sexual harassment rearrange their lives to avoid harassment. For example, they take different pathways to get to class, delete online profiles, or change their phone numbers. Ignoring harassment will not make it go away. Furthermore, changing your life is emotionally and physically exhausting and can lead to mental and physical health issues.

Myth: Only women can be victims of sexual harassment. Only men can be sexual harassers.

Fact: This is a dangerous myth. Although the vast majority of victims of sexual harassment are women, anyone can be harassed. Men may be harassed less as a whole, but the percentage of the population of victims of sexual harassment is much higher for gay men than traditionally

(continued on the next page)

Myths & FACTS

masculine straight men. Also, there is a strong likelihood that people in every group, no matter how they identify, underreport sexual harassment.

Myth: Women who are sexually harassed generally provoke harassment by the way they behave, how they dress, or how they look.

Fact: Unfortunately, this idea has long been held by many people in society. While it is slowly beginning to be challenged in society at large, there are still many people who will blame the victim for how she looked. This is referred to as "victim blaming," as well as "asking for it." No one asks to be spoken to or touched simply because she wore a skirt, did her makeup a certain way, or danced at a party. No one has the right to harass anyone else, and everyone has the right to wear what she wants, have fun how she chooses (within the law, of course), and wear her hair or makeup how she wishes.

If You're a Victim of Sexual Harassment

Being sexually harassed is a horrible experience. It can lead to self-doubt, depression, and anxiety. This chapter will explore what you should do if you or someone you know has been the victim of sexual harassment.

Who Can Be a Victim of Sexual Harassment?

As mentioned previously in this resource, anyone can be the victim of sexual harassment. The New York City Alliance Against Sexual Assault published a report stating that 81 percent of students will experience some form of sexual harassment during

Being the victim of sexual harassment can lead to many mental and even physical problems. Don't be afraid to seek help.

their time as a student, and 27 percent of students will experience it often. It is not isolated to just a few students either, as 85 percent of students say that students harass other students. If these statistics weren't bad enough, nearly 40 percent of students report that teachers and school employees sexually harass students in school.

Young people are especially vulnerable to being victims of sexual harassment or assault. Of victims of sexual harassment, 15 percent are ages twelve to seventeen, and 54 percent are between the ages of eighteen and thirty-four. Fortunately, as you age you do become less likely to be a victim. Those sixty-five and older are 92 percent less likely than twelve- to twenty-four-year-olds to be victims. Of tenth and eleventh graders, 61 percent report that they have been sexually harassed at school.

Young women are more likely to be sexually harassed or abused than their male counterparts. Younger women, those between sixteen and nineteen years old, are four times more likely to be victims. Of girls, 43 percent experience unsolicited sexual attention. This can manifest itself in pressure for dates and/or sex. Being pressured into sex is a big warning sign that you are not in a good relationship. You do not have to have sex with someone because he tells you he loves you or as a test to prove that you love someone. According to an article by Dawson McAllister, a student named Becca recalled an experience where she gave in to harassment and had sex. She had this to say: "I was recently violated by a guy who I thought was a really great guy, but then he started pressuring me and now I hate him for it. We aren't even talking anymore. If you're a guy and you read this, can you please take this seriously and please respect the girl that you like and please don't violate her! It can really make a big difference in anyone's life."

Straight young men, too, can be victims of sexual harassment but make up a statistically smaller sample of victims. This is not to say that young men are not harassed more than reported, there is evidence that social pressure makes

While women make up the vast majority of harassment victims, men can be victimized, too. Societal pressures of "being a man" prevent most male victims from reporting their experiences.

straight men of any age even more timid in reporting harassment than any other group. The numbers of harassment climb exponentially for young men who identify as gay.

However, even among gay or bisexual teens, separating young people by gender still shows that young women are more likely to experience harassment. In terms of sexual orientation, 23 percent of heterosexual young men reported being harassed compared to 43 percent of heterosexual young women. Lesbian young women still reported higher percentages than the 66 percent of gay young men and bisexual young women.

Transgender or gender nonconforming teens have the highest rates of sexual harassment. A staggering 81 percent of transgender or gender nonconforming teens report that they have been sexually harassed.

There is also one group not immediately thought of who can be damaged by sexual harassment: those who witness it. Although this is a fairly new area of study, there seems to be evidence that those who routinely witness sexual harassment—most often occurring in schools—might begin to think of sexual harassment as normal. This can create a culture in which sexual harassment is thought to be "part of growing up." This is wrong.

One final note: sexual harassment is not just something that happens to your peers who look a certain way, such as those with large breasts. A fifteen-year-old named Lindsay told Richa Gulati from *Teen Vogue* that when she was in seventh grade, "I was flat-chested when other girls started to develop, and I was told that I wasn't a girl," she says. It was not just her male classmates who were mean to her. She explains, "As I was getting ready for a school dance, girls came up to me to ask how I could hold up my dress when I didn't have breasts and said maybe I was really a lesbian."

The nonstop remarks made her question herself. "They brought insecurity about my body to the surface," Lindsay says. "It can make girls feel like they should do something to prove the comments wrong—like stuffing their bra or going further sexually with a boy than they normally would in order to prove they're a girl."

Harassment in Hollywood

You might think that being an actor is a dream job: exotic locations, adoring fans, lots of money. However, as mentioned earlier, there is no place that is free of sexual harassment. You are not alone if you are concerned about what will happen just because you do not want to date someone. According to an article by Alanna Vagianos for the *Huffington Post*,

(continued on the next page)

Celebrities are not immune to workplace sexual harassment. Actor Anna Camp has worried about whether she would be treated professionally after declining a date from another actor.

(continued from the previous page)

actor Anna Camp explained that her life mirrored the character she was playing in *Good Girls Revolt:* "[I have had moments] on sets where I have been shooting a scene with someone, it's going very well, but I can tell... 'Oh God, is he going to ask me out?' ... And then I have to work with him for the next month. How do I maintain that balance of not offending him, but getting my point across that I don't want to go out on a date?"

The star had this advice to give, "Young girls—stand up. Stop competing with one another and come together and stand up for yourselves in the moment." She continued "I've had times where I was sexually harassed or sexually discriminated against, and I go home and I don't say anything in the moment and I mull over it and I can't go to sleep and I think: 'Why didn't I just stand up for myself?' It's OK to stand up for yourself."

You might think, "If she is afraid to stand up for herself, what can I do?" Take Anna Camp's advice and speak up. You are stronger than you think; don't be afraid to act!

What to Do If You Are Being Harassed

Sexual harassment can occur just about anywhere. A group of female students recently told the *Christian Science Monitor* that, even though they went to a so-called "good" school, they still experienced sexual harassment as freshmen: "Ten or so senior boys would line up at the stair balcony during class change—calling girl's names, trying to look down their shirts, and even spitting on some girls—which was disgusting." The solution was to avoid taking that stairway to class, but was that the best option?

If you are a victim of sexual harassment, you may feel scared, and you may feel like it is you against the world. But there are some immediate, practical steps you can take to help you battle back against this treatment. Remember that each situation is different, however, and there is no one right way when it comes to handling sexual harassment. Some schools are more aware of the problem of teenage sexual harassment, while others, sadly, will sometimes write off sexual harassment as "boys being boys." That being said, the following list of tips should assist you:

• **Tell the harasser to stop**. This may seem extremely obvious, however, it is surprisingly rare that the person who is being harassed tells the harasser to stop. You can do this any of several ways: in person, over text, in an email, or in a letter. If you do write to your harasser, save a copy (save a copy of what you send no mater what means of communication you use). You may need it as evidence later if your harasser does not stop and you opt to report him or her.

- **Tell a trusted adult**. Perhaps you have a favorite teacher or a parent or other relative whom you trust with this kind of information. More and more schools have a staff member who is a dedicated counselor dealing with bullying (and remember, sexual harassment is a form of bullying). Most schools have systems set up to deal with this type of behavior.

- **Keep a journal**. This is extremely important. If your harasser sends you direct messages, whether they are offensive pictures, videos, or texts, save them all. As we learned from the Clarence Thomas confirmation hearings, sexual harassment can come down to "he said, she said." Having evidence that you have been sexually harassed can prove to be vital, especially if legal action must be taken. Write down what happened, who was there (include people who did not harass you), how it made you feel, and what you did. Although it may be painful to recall the events, writing them down

Journals and other forms of documentation are extremely important when you are being sexually harassed. The more information you have to show authorities, the better off you'll be.

can also be a relief. Some victims have described writing as a way to help get the bad events out of their heads.

- **Do not quit!** If the first person you tell does not take you seriously, find another person. If he or she doesn't believe you, tell another person. The adults in your life have a responsibility to protect you from sexual harassment. If they are not taking that responsibility seriously, keep speaking out until you find someone who does.

Take the Sexual Harassment Quiz

You might be uncertain about whether or not you have been sexually harassed or know someone who has. Take this true or false quiz and find out. Grab a sheet of paper and pen or pencil to write down your answers:

1. If a girl wears revealing clothing, it is an invitation for sex.
2. Bullying and sexual harassment are not the same thing.
3. Sexual harassment cannot happen online.
4. Calling someone an offensive name is okay if it is a joke or the person is your friend.
5. If someone says stop, but they are laughing, you don't have to stop.
6. If you kiss someone once, you can do it again.
7. Sexual harassment happens only when a male says something to a female.

(continued on the next page)

(continued from the previous page)

8. It is okay to send nudes to someone if you do it anonymously.
9. Talking about people's bodies is very funny.
10. If someone has done sexual things, it is okay to talk about it.

Hopefully you answered false to all of the previous statements. The following list explains the reasons why each statement is false:

1. There is no such thing as an invitation for sex unless you ask someone to have sex and they clearly answer yes.
2. While not all bullying is sexual harassment, sexual harassment is definitely a form of bullying.
3. More and more, the internet is exactly where the sexual harassment of teens occurs.
4. Offensive words and slurs are not jokes.
5. Sometimes laughing is a strategy people use to cope with a situation. Laughter does not mean the person thinks it is funny.
6. You do not have the right to someone's body, just as no one has the right to yours. Just because something happened once does not mean it can happen whenever one person wants it.

Kissing and any kind of touching should occur only when both people want it to.

7. Anyone can harass anyone, regardless of gender or gender identity. Harassment is about making someone feel uncomfortable, afraid, or shamed, and it is not gender specific.

8. Sending anonymous unrequested nude photos or videos is not okay! Some people who send such pictures prefer to hide their identity because they know it is wrong.

9. Never joke about another person's appearance, whether it is sexual or just something you think is funny. While it may be tempting to make a joke based on how someone looks, it is usually hurtful.

10. Gossip is something we all engage in, but consider this: has anyone ever said something that wasn't true about you? There is a chance your information is wrong. Also, what someone chooses to do with his or her body is not any of your business.

Sexual Harassment and Underreporting

As mentioned previously, the statistics about the frequency of incidents of sexual harassment are never as definite as we would like. When dealing with an emotionally traumatic event like sexual harassment, there is not always a clear indication of what happened when compared to, for example, drunk driving accidents.

Why is sexual harassment underreported in person and online? A 2014 study that took place in Belgium looked to find out by focusing on the online reporting of sexual harassment. Do any of their results sound familiar to you?

- Out of three hundred teens who said they had been sexually harassed online, only sixty (or 20 percent) of students reported the abuse to a social media platform. Only about half received a response, and the content was removed in only eighteen cases. This is extremely dangerous and the fault of the social media hosts. The lack of response to each individual case and the incredibly few actions taken may make you think that nothing will be done, so you may as well not report it to begin with. This is not true. Remember, no one has the right to make you feel harassed, especially when you are trying to enjoy yourself online. If at first you don't get the help you need, keep looking until you do.
- Related to the previous point, many students reported that they were concerned that

It may seem obvious, but reporting harassment, online or otherwise, increases the likelihood that it will stop. Show a trusted adult any posts that harass you.

complaining would not result in anything being done about it. Worse yet, they feared that speaking out would only make matters worse. Given the response rates, this idea is not without reality. However, ignoring harassment will not make it go away. This is not a "don't feed the trolls" situation. This is also not just a case of someone trying to draw you into an argument. This is a situation in which someone is trying to force you to react in a sexual way. Nothing is more personal, and few things are worse than trying to make someone physically afraid.

- Many of those surveyed did not do anything because they thought they were not harassed enough or the harassment was not "severe enough" to call for a report. This is also very dangerous. There is never a time when someone saying something sexual to you is okay if you did not invite him or her to do it. Do not think you have to cope with someone sexually harassing you because it was in the form of a joke as opposed to a more obvious statement. Harassment is harassment.

CHAPTER THREE

How to Help Yourself

I f you are the victim of sexual harassment, you may be completely overwhelmed. You may feel emotionally scarred. Some people must cope with the ramifications from physical violations as well. No matter what happened, coping with sexual harassment is never easy. Always remember, sexual harassment is not your fault. And you have options to help you heal.

The Long-Term Effects of Sexual Harassment

Recently, psychologists have been paying more attention to the long-term effects of sexual harassment on its victims. The results clearly reveal a connection between the physical and mental well-being of victims and their harassment. Just because the event is over does not necessarily

One of the worst parts about sexual harassment is that it can continue to affect you long after it happens. Do not be afraid to seek help.

mean they have moved on. Let's look at some of the most common long-term effects.

Depression

Depression is the most common effect of sexual harassment. This is a serious problem and is probably best addressed with a therapist or counselor. A long-term study found that of one thousand youths who had been sexually harassed in their teens and early twenties, most still show symptoms of depression in their thirties.

Post-Traumatic Stress Disorder (PTSD)

Post-traumatic stress disorder (PTSD) has also been found in numerous studies of sexual harassment victims. One sign that you may be experiencing PTSD is avoiding the people and places that remind you of when you were harassed. Another is reexperiencing the event or experiencing frequent recall of upsetting, disturbing memories of what happened.

Never underestimate just how damaging sexual harassment can be. Consider this: according to a Livescience article by Rachael Rettner, women in the military who have been sexually harassed develop PTSD at a rate of four times that of women who go to combat. To put it another way, many women in the military find combat easier to deal with than sexual harassment.

Suicidal Thoughts

One of the most dangerous effects of sexual harassment is suicidal thoughts. According to the Rachael Rettner article, in a study of one thousand Canadian high school students, 23 percent said they had experienced some form of sexual harassment in the last six months. Of that group, 15 percent said they had made suicide attempts or had thought about suicide, compared to just 2 percent of students who hadn't experienced sexual harassment. Suicide is never a solution to sexual harassment—or any problem, no matter how horrible it seems.

Sleep Problems and Drug Abuse

Another two common long-term effects of sexual harassment are two sides of the same coin: sleep problems and drug abuse. In the case of sleep problems,

The stress and anxiety that result from being a victim of sexual harassment can make it difficult to relax and fall asleep when it is time for bed.

the increased levels of stress and anxiety can create restlessness. Some victims report an inability to sleep at night. They lie awake reliving the events in their heads, which thwarts their ability to relax. Still others have reported that they have such terrible nightmares about when they were harassed that they would prefer not to sleep.

An inability to escape the horrible memories is also one of the major reasons victims turn to drug abuse. Oftentimes people make the mistake of thinking that, for example, someone got really drunk and then something bad happened. But it is just as likely, if not more so, that someone got extremely drunk *because* something bad happened to him or her. Studies have shown that, for example, women in college who drink heavily are more likely to have been victims of sexual harassment (or worse) when they were younger.

Please remember that no matter what happened to you or what the circumstances are, none of the long-term effects are anything to take lightly. Take them seriously. Take yourself seriously. Seek out help or ask someone to help you find the help you need. While one person did something bad to you, do not forget that there are many more people who want to see you become healed, whole, and happy again.

Tragedy in India

Sexual harassment is not contained to any one country or culture. India has begun to have their own national conversation around sexual harassment and the treatment of women. The suicides of two teenage girls who were the victims of sexual harassment from a group of young men on motorcycles has led to street protests and demands for stiffer penalties.

While there has been more attention paid to all cases of violence against women, it is still not changing the nation fast enough. According to an article by Nita Bhalla for Reuters, from 2012 to 2013, reports of crimes against women rose by 26.7 percent. Perhaps this is a reaction to women demanding more respect; either way it is a tragedy.

The two teenage girls left suicide notes at their education center. They warned that more and more girls would kill themselves if the Indian government and society as a whole did not do more to stop and punish sexual harassment. And more importantly, they wrote that the Indian government needed to help change how people view women to prevent it from happening in the first place.

Fortunately for law enforcement in this case, there are some descriptions of the motorcycles as

(continued on the next page)

(continued from the previous page)

well as their registration numbers. Some of the teenage girls' classmates have come forward as witnesses also.

No matter what country you call home, please do not consider suicide an option. Your life is more important and bigger than sexual harassment. Things will get better.

Finding Emotional Support

Many people do not know how to help victims of sexual harassment. Because the damage from sexual harassment is not physical, it can be difficult for people to understand that you are not yourself. They may tell you to move on with your life and to accept what happened. That is easier said than done.

So what can you do? Following is a list containing some options for finding emotional support for you to consider:

- **Talk to people about what happened.** You will be pleasantly surprised that for every person who tells you to move on, there will be even more people who want to listen to your story. It is important to talk about what happened to you. It may be therapeutic for you to express your feelings. And talking about your experience may help others; another victim may realize that he or she is not alone, simply because you shared what happened to you.

- **Do not let others tell you "what really happened."** Nor should you let people tell you how you should deal with being a victim of sexual harassment. We are all different and each situation is unique. There is no one-size-fits-all solution for something as complex as sexual harassment.
- **Join a support group.** There is a good chance that there is a support group near you where people gather together, listen to one another, and help each other heal. Studies of support groups show that people are more likely to accomplish their goals (in this case, recovering from sexual harassment) than by themselves.
- **Write about your experience.** The power of writing has historically been a great way to express yourself. A journal may be a way to articulate your feelings in a private way. You never have to show anyone your words, unless you want to.
- **Get beyond shame or self-blaming.** This is easier said than done and can take a long time for some victims of sexual harassment. When something bad happens to you, it is tempting to think you did something wrong. You didn't. The person who harassed you is the one in the wrong.

If you are battling depression, insomnia, or any other side effects of sexual harassment, speak to a mental health professional.

- **Try to grow your social circle in a positive way.** Perhaps when you were being harassed, a friend didn't believe you. It may be time to find a new friend to confide in. A true friend will believe you and support you, especially when it comes to something as important as your emotional well-being and physical safety. Make sure you surround yourself with friends who support you and have your best interests in mind.
- **Therapy or counseling may be an option.** This will require an adult who is willing to help you with some research. Find a place that has access to a therapist who understands what victims who have been sexually harassed are experiencing. Only now is the therapist community beginning to understand the long-term effects that sexual harassment can have on teens. If you cannot find someone trained or experienced in this area, a sexual assault or abuse counselor may be a good place to start.

Legal Action

Some victims of sexual harassment decide that they wish to take their harasser to court. Taking legal action is a big step, and not everyone is prepared to take it. But for some, seeing their case through the justice system gives them satisfaction and closure.

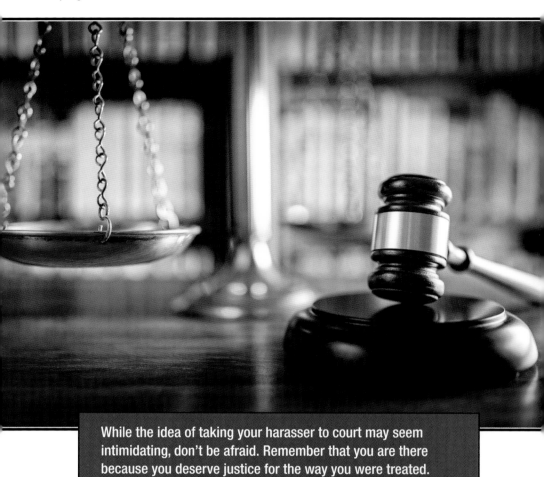

While the idea of taking your harasser to court may seem intimidating, don't be afraid. Remember that you are there because you deserve justice for the way you were treated.

Maybe you are a victim of sexual harassment at school, and you have told someone and nothing is happening. Or perhaps you told someone and the pain is too great. Whatever your circumstances, you may decide to go to court. What happens next depends greatly on whether or not the person who harassed you is an adult or fellow teenager.

When an adult who works for the school harasses you, generally the school district is sued. The idea is that the adult is a representative of the school district and therefore the school district is responsible. The worry with this strategy is that unless supervisors at the district level knew about it and there is hard evidence, a verdict in your favor will depend greatly upon many circumstances beyond your control. It is also common for the victim to sue the school official who harassed them. Again, evidence plays a key role—so keep that journal and all the messages and gather witnesses. Many victims have had success with this route.

If another student is harassing you, things can get very complex very quickly. An article by Alexandra Yoon-Hendricks for the *Daily Californian* offers one example. In 2016, a sixteen-year-old Berkeley High School student sued the school district for not properly handling her case. The lawsuit said that she had been persistently stalked and harassed by a male student. He would catcall, stalk, and make sexual comments like "look at that butt." He also called her his girlfriend even though they were not dating. (Remember that sexual harassment is rarely about sex and more about power. There is no better illustration than someone claiming you are his or her partner and taking away your ability to choose.)

In October 2015, things got even worse. She claimed the male student grabbed her buttocks in physical education class. The victim filled out a statement and spoke with the vice principal (which is the right thing to do!), but the vice principal failed to notify the director of student services and the on-campus police officer, which was against district policy.

The day after, the victim and her mother met with the vice principal and a police official. The police official did not act properly, allegedly asking the victim, "Why didn't you report him earlier?" and suggesting that the student invited the predatory behavior by not behaving properly.

Shocked, the victim asked that the harasser be arrested and charged, to which the police official said, "We are trying to keep these young men out of the system."

A few days later, the victim was harassed again, and she had to shove the young man away as he attempted to hug her. She was so upset by all of this that she didn't attend school for more than a month.

When she finally returned to school, specific routes to class were given to both the harassed student and the harassing student. The victim was also promised an escort to class, but the school never came through with one.

Sadly, things still did not improve and she ran into the harasser at the BART station (Bay Area Rapid

Transit, the regional rail service in the San Francisco Bay Area). When she asked the principal's assistant how she could be safe if they kept seeing each other, she was asked why she continued to attend Berkeley High School if she was having such problems.

The student from Berkeley High School did everything right. She reported the incident to school officials, for example, and she told her mother. But the system designed to protect her failed. So she decided to hire a lawyer and take her case to court. As of this publication, the suit was still in progress and had not yet been settled.

Although plenty of sexual harassment occurs online, the law has not currently adjusted quickly enough to cover these types of situations. But your actions should still be the same, no matter how or where you were sexually harassed. Document the incidents, report the incidents, and do not give up until you are satisfied with the outcome.

10 Great Questions to Ask a Campus Safety Official

Depending on your school, some of these questions may not apply, however, these questions are a good starting point if you are researching your school, a new school, or perhaps later at a college or university. The more you know before something happens, the easier it will be to cope should something unfortunate occur.

1. Where can I find the school's policy on sexual harassment?

2. Does the school admit there is a problem with sexual harassment?

3. What are the punishments for people who sexually harass other students? Expulsion? Suspension? Is it left to law enforcement?

4. Can students report harassment anonymously?

5. Does the school enforce no-contact orders?

6. What is the policy for missing school as a result of being a victim of sexual harassment?

7. Does the school have or allow student organizations to educate people about and stop sexual violence?

8. Are there any staff members or counselors who are trained to deal specifically with teenage sexual harassment?

9. If sexual harassment has occurred, does the school have services on the school grounds for helping victims?

10. What additional resources are available in the community for victims of sexual harassment?

CHAPTER FOUR

Technology and Harassment

As the websites and apps that teens use are constantly changing—fewer teens use Facebook than ever before—many of the adults who want to help you are having a harder time keeping up. According to Teensafe.com, in 1995, 50 percent of teens were online every day. Teens were watching an average of two-and-a-half hours of MTV every day, and there were only 23,500 websites. In 2005, 87 percent of teens were online daily, mostly sending emails or playing games. Myspace was the most popular social media website, Facebook was only one year old, and there were 64.8 million websites. In 2015, 95 percent of teens were online daily, phone calls have been replaced by text messages, 81 percent of teens were using social media, and the number of websites had ballooned to 1.2 billion.

Technology, and the apps we use, are constantly evolving. As we continue to spend more and more time online, the opportunities for online harassment increase as well.

Harassment Online

Sadly, issues such as sexual harassment, along with other real-life problems, have followed teens online. The same statistical trends about in-person sexual harassment also exist on the internet. A Pew Research Center survey of more than one thousand teenagers between the ages of thirteen and seventeen years old found that 35 percent of teen girls have had to block a user from one of their accounts compared to only 16 percent of boys.

In Baltimore, Maryland, a young man repeatedly asked a young woman out. She was not interested and tried to be nice about letting him know. When he persisted, she was forced to be more direct. Not only did she say no but she also told him not to contact her anymore. After she blocked his phone number, he used a website to send anonymous text messages. (Many websites

Blocking someone who harasses may provide more peace of mind. While it doesn't solve the problem, it may be better than feeling scared each time you get a text.

exist to help users send anonymous messages, and it is legal to do.) She tried to change her phone number, but her smartphone carrier would charge a fee in order to do so. He also launched a multiplatform attack, which involved posting her phone number on Instagram, Twitter, and Facebook. Fortunately, she knew to take the steps discussed earlier in this resource. She began to gather evidence of the online harassment and took him to court. Unfortunately, this story illustrates how a determined harasser can use technology to make the person being harassed always uncomfortable, always on guard.

What Are Teenagers Sharing Online?

In the Baltimore, Maryland, example, the harasser used the knowledge of the woman's phone number to harass her. Often times, as young people—especially young women—share information about their lives online, that information is used against them.

Photos of themselves: Selfies and "usies" (group selfies) are on the rise. There is nothing wrong with

Capturing memories with your friends is so much fun. Just be careful of your privacy settings if you post them online.

taking a photo of yourself and posting it online. In fact, selfies are the most common items posted on social media by teens. However, teens need to be careful of their privacy settings. Harassers can use these photos. And be especially careful if your friends list or your followers contain strangers.

Their school name: Again, there is nothing wrong with having school pride. However, by posting your school name, you advertise certain telling facts:

(continued on the next page)

(continued from the previous page)

that you are a teenager and also where you will be for six or seven hours a day Monday through Friday.

Their relationship status: If you are in a relationship, how you choose to talk about it on social media is up to you. There are, though, a few things to keep in mind before you share too much information. If you are single, harassers may look at this as an invitation to get you into a conversation and push to take it to a sexual level. If you are in a relationship, some people may try to pry into your intimate life and find out if you are sexually active.

Videos of themselves: The content of videos can vary widely and so will the attention they bring. For example, predators might not be very interested in seeing your school band recital, however, a public video of you dancing in your room could bring unwanted attention. Again, it is okay to post these videos. If you learned a new dance move and want to show it off for your family and friends, that's great, but just be aware of your privacy settings.

Remember, once something is on the internet, it's there forever. You can never completely erase it. Be smart about what you post and pay attention to who will see it.

To Block or Not to Block

Today's teens often wish they did not have to have social media. Some of them even think it is ruining their lives, but if they did not have it, then they would feel isolated. One such person is Christina, who lives in Austin, Texas. Only fifteen years old, she repeatedly negotiated advances made by an older boy. Like the young woman from Baltimore discussed earlier, he followed her around across multiple social networks.

Talking about the situation, Christina said, "He liked me around five years ago, and he still does. It's uncomfortable because he'll make new accounts just to see what I'm up to, because I don't like setting myself private on anything. But I would block him, and he'll make another account to see me. And he'll make another one. And it's been going on since sixth grade."

Additionally, whenever Christina posts selfies, her teenage harasser would screenshot them and post them to Snapchat. She figures he has quite the collection.

Then the stalking and harassing behavior switched from online to real life. He sent her a message that he was going to her house. Christina replied that he shouldn't go there, and her family wasn't even home. But he didn't listen to her request and went to her house anyway. However, she did not feel that this was enough to make her want to talk to an adult or counselor. Instead, she blocked him and made another account.

You might think that because posts only last for twenty-four hours on apps like Snapchat that you are safe, but screen shots live forever.

While it is tempting to block someone and/or create a new account, there is a problem with this. Namely, teenage girls begin to think that the behavior of their harassers is normal and a problem for them to handle on their own. Unfortunately, this approach ignores the bigger problem of males thinking that they have a right to a female's time, attention, physical space, or body. To think of it another way, while blocking someone potentially creates a safe space for you, it does not change the actions of the person harassing you. For this type of behavior to change, the person has to be reported. Always report this behavior to a parent or trusted adult, even if the actions or comments seem like they are no big deal. If it makes you the least bit uncomfortable, tell an adult.

Gamer Harassment

How did female video game developer Zoë Quinn become the target of online harassment? Simple. In 2014, Quinn's angry ex-boyfriend Eron Gjoni wrote a long blog post in which he claimed that she cheated on him. Additionally, he said that people in the video game industry and the media traded sex with her for development opportunities and positive press coverage. Even though these events were

(continued on the next page)

(continued from the previous page)

proven to be false, and the blog post alone is sexual harassment, a controversy about her raged online.

What was one man's grudge against his ex-girlfriend quickly grew as people with connections to sites like 4chan began to attack female journalist Anita Sarkeesian, a self-described feminist writer. Shortly after that, journalist Jenn Frank and game designer Mattie Brice both quit their jobs because of harassment. Additionally, games developer Brianna Wu came under attack.

All the women mentioned received numerous death threats, threats to their families, and some were even told they would be raped—all over social media, Twitter in particular. Both Quinn and Wu had their phone numbers and addresses made public, for example. The threats were so extreme that they both left their houses. They no longer felt safe in their own homes.

Information about a woman's sex life (or supposed sex life) that was posted on the internet led to an organized effort by anonymous strangers acting together to physically and sexually harass people. With the power to change someone's life with a single mouse click, what we post is extremely important and should always be carefully considered. Taking care is important not just for your own physical and mental safety, but also for the physical and mental safety of others.

Protecting Yourself Online and Your Devices

Between your smartphone, computer, and tablet, there are many places where your information and media (pictures, texts, etc.) can easily be stolen. This may make them fair game for harassers. There are some basic steps you can take to make your social media accounts less tempting for potential harassers. While it is unfortunate that we live in a world where you have to think about what you post, there are some things to consider when dealing with your social media accounts.

- **Manage your privacy settings**: This is the most basic thing you can do to help protect yourself. Nearly every social media outlet allows you to control your privacy settings. It is in your best interest to set everything to private or friends only. While it may seem silly, this prevents strangers from discovering you and being in a situation where someone who you think is interested in you turns out to have much worse intentions. On Instagram, for example, it is easy to set your account to private. This allows you to approve everyone who follows you and prevents your photos from being public. While everyone wants to have more followers, be smart about it.

- **Do not become "friends" with people you do not know**: For example, on Facebook, you might get a friend request from someone you do not know. Check to see if you have mutual friends. If you do, ask them about the person. If you do not have any mutual friends, ignore their request.

- **Never respond to inappropriate requests, report them**: Many teens, especially teenage girls, receive inappropriate messages online. These can range from the seemingly innocent, such as questions about what you like, to the truly disgusting, like requests for nude photos. If someone you do not know starts asking questions about your personal life, ask yourself "Why are they asking me this and what can they do with this information?" The last thing you want to do is to provide a would-be predator with volunteered information. Do not reply to these messages. Facebook, for example, makes it easy to report inappropriate contact.

- **Avoid posting or sending inappropriate or sexual pictures and comments**: Like gaining more followers, getting lot of "likes" is a quick and easy way to feel like you are important in the world. Also, expressing your sexuality is something you have the right to do, but it is best done in private. If you post it on social media, even if your account is set to private, it can be hacked, forwarded to other people, or copied. (Later in this chapter you will learn how to protect your accounts from hackers.) Say you send a photo to a partner while you are in a relationship. If the two of you break up, your ex could use that picture against you. Another way to look at this is to think about if you'd be embarrassed if people such as your grandparents, best friend's parents, or teachers saw it, reconsider sending or posting it.

When it comes to how to protect your account passwords and devices, Karen S., who has worked in New York City's bustling tech start-up scene for more than eight years and has led workshops on protecting yourself online, has some tips. In an interview with the author, she had this to say about online protection, "At every tech company I've worked for, we took security very seriously. We encrypt messages and use password managers. While there aren't millions of dollars at stake for personal users, the general public, and teenagers especially, should take steps to protect their devices and their accounts."

She offered the following six tips to help prevent harassers from stealing your identity or information and then using it against you:

1. **Create a unique password for each account and each device.** While this may sound like a lot of work, you can use a free password manager

like LastPass. "I know it seems inconvenient to have different passwords for each site you use," said Karen, "but it is worth it to have this extra layer of security. Think of it like a big boat. They have separate chambers with walls in between so if one chamber springs a leak, the entire boat won't be filled with water."

2. **Create a better password**. When it comes to passwords, you never want to make them anything obvious. Avoid things like your birthday (or that of anyone in your family or friends), the name of your school, and things of this sort. These passwords are not difficult to figure out. Instead, you should create a longer password, something at least fifteen characters long. Sound difficult? It isn't. Websites like xkcd.com offer all sorts of tips. Often times, four random words stuck together will do the trick. Of course, some websites require special characters, but do not create a pattern. If you saw the movie *The Imitation Game,* you know that Alan Turing was able to crack the Germans' code in Word War II because they always ended their messages with an obvious phrase.

3. **Lock your device every time you walk away from it**. "This, like everything else, does add an extra step for you, but it also adds another layer of protection from people who might want to steal

12:54
Friday 05 July

🔒

Slide to unlock

It may seem inconvenient, but locking your devices each time you walk away from them can save you from all sorts of trouble.

your data. People who are motivated to harass you could be motivated to steal information from your devices," said Karen. This is especially important, say, in a school, which is where most teen harassment begins. For your phone or tablet, it is better to create a two-step process that requires both a fingerprint and a password. Some computers allow you to set up "hot corners" so each time you place the cursor in the designated corner, your computer will automatically lock. It can take only a moment of distraction, say getting up to talk to a friend in a computer lab, to put everything at risk.

4. **Be selective about which wireless networks you join**. "While data use can be a concern, it is nothing compared to the headache of having your accounts hacked," said Karen. Sure, it can be great to find a Wi-Fi hotspot, but you need to be careful. Make sure it is a network that you know. Also, do not always have Wi-Fi enabled on your phone, otherwise you might join a network that is bad and not even know it!

5. **Turn off location settings on your device**. Karen said that she tells people, "Whether it is for photos, or anything else, turn your location setting off. Some apps may say they can't work when location is disabled, but often if you hit

ignore, the app will work just fine." Not only does this help protect your device, but it also protects you. Remember, one way harassers may harass you is by showing up where you are. Not only can this cause mental discomfort, but it can also put you in physical harm.

6. **Set up a remote wiping system**. This advanced step essentially allows you to reset your phone from a different device if someone should ever steal it. Consider talking to your parents or guardian about setting up this option.

CHAPTER FIVE

How to Be an Ally

Perhaps you have never experienced sexual harassment in your own life. Count yourself fortunate! As you have read, sexual harassment can occur in many places, anyone can be a victim, and the effects can be traumatic. This does not mean that you cannot be helpful to those who are victims of sexual harassment or that you are powerless to help stop sexual harassment.

What can you do? Become an ally. In many social justice circles, the term "ally" has come to mean someone who is not directly touched by issues such as racism and misogyny but still acts to assist those who are affected. One example is a white person showing up and participating in a Black Lives Matter protest.

Young Men

Recently, celebrity Ariana Grande encountered a fan while she was out with her boyfriend. The man

Singer and actress Ariana Grande recently was objectified by a fan when she was out with her boyfriend. Never talk about a person like they are an object.

was incredibly excited to meet her, but his behavior could be considered harassment. He talked about how "Ariana is sexy as hell, man!" and then congratulated her boyfriend for having a sexual relationship with her. This way of talking about Grande made her an object and not a person.

As we have read throughout this resource, although anyone can be harassed—women, men, and people from all minority groups, including LGBTQ+— women of all ages are disproportionately targeted for sexual harassment. Perhaps, as a young man, reading about sexual harassment makes you wonder what you can do to help. Maybe as you read you want to come up with ways to help stop the culture of toxic masculinity that allows the sexual harassment of women to occur. Or perhaps you wonder what you could do if you, like Grande's boyfriend, heard another man speaking about a woman you care about, whether it's a partner, family member, friend, or acquaintance. Below are four tips designed just for you!

1. **Listen to your female and minority friends**. They are the ones who experience this, and they are the ones to tell you what happened. As you listen to their stories, you can learn to identify sexual harassment when it happens. As we have learned, it is not always as obvious as someone getting her butt grabbed.

Being an ally doesn't always mean being a hero. Sometimes, just checking on someone to make sure they are OK can be its own kind of heroism.

2. **Ask "Are you okay?"** This might sound easier to do than it actually is. If your friend is being harassed right in front of you or you suspect that she is, ask her, "Are you okay?" If she answers no or you think she might be scared to say yes, stay with her, and, if you feel like it is safe to do so, stand between your friend and the person harassing. Again, sexual harassment is about power, and often the harasser might be afraid to continue if you are standing between your friend and the harasser. Be sure to keep both your friend and yourself safe from harm if at all possible.

3. **After you know your friend is okay, tell the harasser to stop**. Turn from your friend and try to be brave enough to tell the harasser to stop. It is important to note that you are not looking to get into a fight. Your goal is to get him to leave and for the situation to end peacefully. Also, if you start a fight with the harasser, you may get into trouble. Then the harasser can claim that he is the victim, which only creates new problems for you and lets the person who is actually wrong off the hook.

4. **Include more people**. Because the type of sexual harassment we are talking about is occurring in real life, chances are that it will be in a public or community space. While you confront the harasser, speak with confidence and call on others to talk about what they see. They may be just

as upset as you but unwilling to speak unless called upon. Get involved. If more people say that the sexual harassment is unacceptable, the less likely it is that the harasser will continue. And perhaps he will think twice about doing it again in the future.

Additionally, there are many men of all ages who are ignorant about sexual harassment. This makes sense, as sexual harassment rarely happens to straight cisgender males. If they are willing to listen, patiently explain the facts about sexual harassment, whom it happens to, and the statistics. You might just make the world a better place! (You do not want to get involved in an exchange with someone, such as an internet troll, who is just looking to cause problems. Even though it can be tempting, it's not worth your time. And you might just make yourself a target for harassment yourself.)

Toxic Masculinity

The phrase "toxic masculinity" has recently become quite popular. A quick Google search shows nearly eighteen thousand articles on the topic, both arguing that it is a problem, and others, sadly, arguing that it

(continued on the next page)

(continued from the previous page)

is something that has been made up. But what is it?

Simply put, toxic masculinity is the idea that boys are raised with certain ideas that create the society that we live in. These ideas include things like thinking that sexual harassment is normal and that "boys will be boys," or that certain behaviors, usually bad behaviors such as bullying, are acceptable for males, just because they are, well, male.

Some of the ways that young men are exposed to toxic masculinity is, for example, when they are young and crying and then told to "man up" and not cry. It is okay to be emotional. Also included in toxic masculinity is the idea that men need to have as many sexual partners as possible and that being a man includes and even encourages violence.

While scholars and researchers are still working on the details, there is growing acceptance that how society raises boys can negatively affect how they act once they are men. Think of it as society's version of peer pressure.

Easy Steps Anyone Can Take

Chances are there is a girl at your school who has physically developed faster than her classmates, and now she is getting harassed for her larger chest. Or

Being a teenager is already hard, but feeling like you are alone and no one cares makes it harder. Try sitting with someone new at lunch.

maybe there is a boy who does not act tough enough, and people are harassing him thinking that he is gay. Maybe another student is going through a gender transition. There are things you can do to make all of these people feel like they are not alone and that harassment is not okay. For example, just being with them can make a world of difference. Often times, victims of sexual harassment think they are alone. So consider joining them during lunch, free time like study hall, or physical education class. The times at school when they are not in a classroom setting are often when your peers are most vulnerable, and then they become targets for harassers.

Follow the models in the examples for young men discussed previously. Say something to the person who is harassing your schoolmate. Of course, try to do it in a way that does not make the situation worse, but often simply telling someone what he is doing is wrong is enough to make the bully stop.

Finally, always tell an adult at school what is happening.

HeartMob

Since 2005, a group of leaders from Hollaback! (an organization dedicated to stopping catcalling) received numerous harassing emails. It started with gay slurs and eventually they began to receive rape and death threats. In 2013, a new group was formed called HeartMob.

HeartMob has the simple goal of helping people who are experiencing online harassment (sexual or otherwise). In real life, sometimes people are not around to help when someone is being harassed, but online help can be a share or retweet away. The ability to get a large group of people together quickly, even virtually, to stop online harassment is extremely powerful. This is especially true when someone is alone in his or her room and it feels like the online harassment is unstoppable.

With HeartMob you can document and report harassment across a variety of platforms and apps. It allows you to ask for the kind of help you need. It is a simple three-step process. First, you tell your story of your online harassment experience, complete with details and examples, on a secure, moderated platform. Then you have the option of selecting allies from people in your life or vetted people in the HeartMob community. Finally, you begin to get the support you need with messages of understanding, resources that may be available to you, and real-life assistance in handling online sexual harassment.

While some continue to believe that harassment of any sort is just "part of the internet," HeartMob disagrees. Everyone has the right to an internet experience free of harassment just as they do in real life. HeartMob writes on their website: "It is not your responsibility to accept harassment for using the internet; it is the responsibility of harassers not to harass you."

What About Activism?

In March 2016, a group of students at Tualatin High School in Oregon began posting anonymously on the web page Project Girls With Guts. They all had one thing in common: they did not feel that the school's administration was taking their claims of sexual harassment and assault seriously enough. Some had never even told school officials because they felt ashamed about what had happened to them. Fortunately, a few students who had had these experiences started talking and then the circle grew as they found more and more students who had also experienced sexual harassment or even assault.

A young man (no names are used because they are

Your peers are a great resource. Many of them will have had similar experiences, and you may be surprised at the strategies they've developed.

all minors) was accused by two separate students of assault, and the response the students received from a counselor in a meeting was, "You have to remember that accusations are just accusations." It was clear that the school was not going to help them. The students were told that if they did not want to have any interaction with the student, they would have to avoid him. So the students began to take action.

Angi Coleman was in a unique position to help. This former Tualatin student had moved to Florida, so she was able to assist her friends at Tualatin without worry about the school pressuring her or anyone getting upset—she lived across the country. In Coleman's own words: "The problem with some girls at Tualatin being as open as I can be, is that they're at risk for getting expelled whereas since I don't go there, I don't have that risk." She used her Twitter account to put out a call to her former classmates for their experiences with sexual harassment at the school. Within days, twenty-four students had replied, some of whom had not even told their parents what had happened to them.

Students in the school's Advocates for Gender Equality club have since combined forces with nearby Sherwood High School's Club Fem for an event called Speak Up—Raising Awareness of Sexual Assault.

This is a wonderful example of what you could do at your school or in your community. Students have traditionally organized in America to bring about change. Now, with more access to information and more communication channels, young people can work within their schools to demand change and provide education or just a safe space for people to discuss their experiences. Does your school have such an organization? If not, consider starting your own club to do this type of work. As mentioned previously, sexual harassment comes out of bullying culture, and peer-to-peer work is often more effective than hoping school administrators can take care of things. Nevertheless, always be respectful and discuss your concerns with administrators.

Be a Friend

Often when someone has been sexually harassed, like with many other things in life, the first person he or she tells is a close friend. If a friend shares with you that he or she has been sexually harassed, you have a powerful responsibility and can affect how your friend begins to cope with what happened. A friend may tell you right away or months later; either way your number-one responsibility is to listen.

Listening is one of the greatest gifts you can give a friend. Make sure you don't interrupt, and respect what they want to do next.

As you have learned, the effect that sexual harassment has on victims can be life changing. They may experience anxiety, shock, anger, sadness, shame, or any combination of these feelings. They might even wonder if it is their fault. When listening to their story, try to keep these things in mind:

- **Believe the victim**. They have been through something horrible. Even if you have doubts, now is not the time to express them. Your friend has experienced a violation and they need to know that you are there for them.
- **Put your emotions to the side**. However you are feeling—and anger is a perfectly appropriate

response—the most important emotions are the victim's emotions. You will have time to process the events in time, but your complete attention should be given to the victim.

- **Support your friend**. Your friend is not at fault. No one hopes to be a victim of sexual harassment. Recall that your friend may be blaming himself or herself for what happened.

  After your friend has told you what happened, do some research and find ways that you can help. At the end of this book is a list of organizations and websites where you can find resources to help your friend when he or she needs you the most!

Glossary

awkward Causing or involving embarrassment.

catcalling People saying or doing inappropriate things, such as whistling or commenting, to others when they are in public; often of a sexual nature.

chaperone Someone, often a parent or teacher, who makes sure a group of people are safe when they go out.

consent To agree to something or give permission for something to occur.

encrypt To put information into secret codes to prevent unapproved viewing.

exponentially More and more quickly or at a greater rate.

firestorm An event that causes great excitement or arguments.

gray area A situation in which right and wrong are unclear or hard to judge.

intuitive Decided to be true by instinct.

lewd Offensive in a sexual way.

lynching Killing someone, usually by hanging from a tree, and without a trial; historically closely associated with the hangings of African Americans.

manifest To demonstrate or show.

misogyny The hatred of or prejudice against women.

movie trailer An advertisement or short introduction to a movie. Also known as a movie preview.

overtones Hints toward something without actually saying what one means.

safe space A place where a person or group of people (for example, LGBTQ+ people) can feel confident they won't be exposed to emotional or physical harm.

sexual predator Someone who tries to have, or has had, sexual contact with another person in an abusive manner.

slut shaming Saying nasty things about someone for the sexual acts they have engaged in.

statistical Relating to statistics, which is the science of collecting and studying data.

traumatic Emotionally upsetting or shocking.

unsolicited Not asked for; offered voluntarily.

verdict A decision made by a court of law.

vetted Have done critical research, such as of a person to make sure he or she is to be trusted.

vital Absolutely crucial or necessary.

For More Information

Alternative—Girl World

Alternatives, Inc.

4730 N. Sheridan

Chicago, IL 60640

Website: https://www.alternativesyouth.org/
programs/girl-world

Facebook: @AlternativesYouth

Instagram: @AlternativesInc

Twitter: @AlternativesInc

YouTube: AlternativesYouthChi

Girl World encourages and supports young women
"to develop leadership skills, explore their college
and career options, and learn about the importance
of positive decisions and healthy relationships."

Girls for Gender Equity

30 3rd Avenue #104

Brooklyn, NY 11217

(718) 857-2239

Email: media@ggenyc.org

Website: http://www.ggenyc.org

Facebook: @GirlsForGenderEquity

Twitter: @GGENYC

YouTube: @GGENYC

Girls for Gender Equity "believes that widespread violence against women and girls of color points to deeply rooted racial and gender discrimination that must be tackled as a peace-building and human rights priority."

Men Stopping Violence

2785 Lawrenceville Highway, Suite 112

Decatur, GA 30033

(404) 270-9894

Website: http://menstoppingviolence.org

Facebook: @MenStoppingViolence

Twitter: @MenStopViolence

The mission of Men Stopping Violence is to get men together in an effort "to end male violence against women and girls through innovative trainings, programs and advocacy." They believe that analyzing the interconnection of all kinds of oppression and working for social justice is the only way to end violence against women and girls.

METRAC

158 Spadina Road

Toronto, ON M5R 2T8

Canada

(416) 392-3135

Email: info@metrac.org

Website: http://www.metrac.org

Facebook: @METRACorg

Twitter: METRACorg

METRAC seeks to modify concepts, endeavors, and approaches to help put an end to violence against women and youth. They encourage security, fairness, and objectivity through teaching and prevention.

National Women's Law Center

11 Dupont Circle NW, Suite 800

Washington, DC 20036

(202) 588-5185

Email: info@nwlc.org

Website: http://nwlc.org

Facebook: @NWLC

Twitter: @NWLC

YouTube: NWLCmedia

The National Women's Law Center works to protect and advance the progress of women and girls at work, in school, and in virtually every aspect of their lives.

Stop Sexual Assault in Schools

1631 NE Broadway Street, #331

Portland, OR 97232

Email: info@stopsexualassaultinschools.org

Website: http://stopsexualassaultinschools.org

Facebook: @StopSexualAssaultInHighSchool

Tumblr: stopsexualassaultinschools.tumblr.com

Twitter: @SSAISorg

The Stop Sexual Assault in Schools (SSAIS) organization seeks to instruct students, families, and schools that all education should be equal for everyone and free from sexual harassment, sexual assault, and gender discrimination.

Women in Cities International

465, rue Saint-Jean, bureau 803

Montréal, QC H2Y 2R6

Canada

(514) 861-6123

Website: http://femmesetvilles.org

Facebook: WomenInCitiesInternational

Instagram: @Women_In_Cities_Intl

Twitter: @WICI_FVI

Women in Cities International believes that women

are their own best resource for what needs to be done to protect them in public spaces. Since 2010, they have been partners in the Because I am a Girl Urban Programme, which has helped to build safe spaces for all kinds of young girls.

Websites

Because of the changing nature of internet links, Rosen Publishing has developed an online list of websites related to the subject of this book. This site is updated regularly. Please use this link to access this list:

http://www.rosenlinks.com/COP/Harass

For Further Reading

Brezina, Corona. *Helping a Friend Who Is Being Bullied*. New York, NY: Rosen Publishing, 2017.

Culp, Jennifer. *I Have Been Sexually Abused. Now What?* New York, NY: Rosen Publishing, 2015.

Gitlin, Martin. *Helping a Friend in an Abusive Relationship*. New York, NY: Rosen Publishing, 2017.

Hamilton, Tracy Brown. *Combatting Internet Shaming*. New York, NY: Rosen Publishing, 2017.

Harasymiw, Therese. *Cyberbullying and the Law*. New York, NY: Rosen Central, 2012.

Henneberg, Susan. *I Have Been Raped. Now What?* New York, NY: Rosen Publishing, 2016.

Jacquet, Jennifer. *Is Shame Necessary?* New York, NY: Pantheon Books, 2015.

Klein, Rebecca T. *Transgender Rights and Protections*. New York, NY: Rosen Publishing, 2017.

Leavitt, Amie. *Combatting Toxic Online Communities*. New York, NY: Rosen Publishing, 2017.

Lindeen, Mary. *Digital Safety Smarts: Preventing Cyberbullying*. Minneapolis, MN: Lerner Classroom, 2016.

McAneney, Caitie. *I Have Been Cyberbullied. Now What?* New York, NY: Rosen Publishing, 2016.

Meyer, Susan. *Combatting "Slut" Shaming.* New York, NY: Rosen Publishing, 2017.

Orr, Tamra B. *I Have Been Shamed on the Internet. Now What?* New York, NY: Rosen Publishing, 2017.

Peterson, Judy Monroe. *How to Beat Cyberbullying.* New York, NY: Rosen Central, 2012.

Schwartz, Heather. *Cyberbullying.* North Mankato, MN: Capstone Press, 2013.

Bibliography

Bhalla, Nita. "Schoolgirls Commit Suicide Over Sexual Harassment." Reuters, August 26, 2014. http://in.reuters.com/article/womensrights-india-suicide-idINKBN0GQ0WO20140826.

Bidwell, Allie. "Study: Sexual Harassment Frequent Among Middle School Students." *U.S. News and World Report*, April 6, 2014. https://www.usnews.com/news/articles/2014/04/06/study-sexual-harassment-frequent-among-middle-school-students.

CBS News. "Anita Hill vs. Clarence Thomas: The Backstory." October 20, 2010. http://www.cbsnews.com/news/anita-hill-vs-clarence-thomas-the-backstory.

Cruz, Eliel. "7 Things Men Can Do to Stop Sexual Harassment." *Teen Vogue*, December 29, 2016. http://www.teenvogue.com/story/how-men-can-stop-sexual-harassment.

FreeAdvice Legal. "Can a Student Sue for Sexual Harassment at School?" Retrieved March 27, 2017. http://law.freeadvice.com/government_law/education_law/school_sexual_harrassment.htm.

Gibson, Caitlin. "Teens Rarely Report Online Harassment. When They Do, They Rarely Get Help." *Washington Post*, February 18, 2016. https://www.washingtonpost.com/news/the-intersect/wp/2016/02/18/teens-rarely-report-online-harassment-when-they-do-they-rarely-get-help/?utm_term=.2cb18376a384.

Gulati, Richa. "How to Deal with Sexual Harassment." *Teen Vogue*, February 3, 2013. http://www.teenvogue.com/story/sexual-harassment-at-school.

Health Enews Staff. "Teens' Sexual Identity Raises Harassment Rates." Advocate Health Care, October 28, 2013. http://www.ahchealthenews.com/2013/10/28/teens-sexual-identity-gender-raise-sexual-harassment-rates.

Iovino, Joe. "Sexual Misconduct at Church: What Every Member Should Know." United Methodist Communications, June 9, 2015. http://www.umc.org/what-we-believe/sexual-misconduct-at-church-what-every-member-should-know.

Kain, Erik. "GamerGate: A Closer Look at the Controversy Sweeping Video Games." *Forbes*, September 4, 2014. https://www.forbes.com/sites/erikkain/2014/09/04/gamergate-a-closer-look-at-the-controversy-sweeping-video-games/#6ac27c4b34f8.

Kids Health. "Sexual Harassment and Sexual Bullying." The Nemours Foundation. Retrieved March 1, 2017. http://kidshealth.org/en/teens/harassment.html.

Kingkade, Tyler. "Students Refuse to Stay Silent About Their High School's Sexual

Assault Response." *Huffington Post*, April 15, 2016. http://www.huffingtonpost.com/entry/tualatin-high-school-sexual-assault_us_570bf2f2e4b0885fb50dbd54.

Kleeman, Sophie. "One Third of Teen Girls Have Been Forced to Block Creeps on the Internet." Mic Network Inc., October 3, 2015. https://mic.com/articles/126173/teenage-girls-face-online-harassment-early-and-often-new-pew-study-shows#.kbTC3LD2b.

Madden, Mary, Amanda Lenhart, Sandra Cortesi, Urs Gasser, Maeve Duggan, Aaron Smith, and Meredith Beaton. "Teens, Social Media, and Privacy." Pew Research Center, May 21, 2013. http://www.pewinternet.org/2013/05/21/teens-social-media-and-privacy.

McAllister, Dawson. "Are You Being Pressured Into Having Sex?" TheHopeLine. Retrieved March 27, 2017. https://www.thehopeline.com/being-pressured-sex.

New York City Alliance Against Sexual Assault. "Fact Sheets: Sexual Harassment for Teens." Retrieved March 27, 2017. http://www.svfreenyc.org/survivors_factsheet_60.html.

RAINN. "Victims of Sexual Violence." Retrieved March 27, 2017. https://www.rainn.org/statistics/victims-sexual-violence.

Rettner, Rachael."6 Ways Sexual Harassment Damages Women's Health." Live Science, November 9, 2011. http://www.livescience. com/16949-sexual-harassment-health-effects. html.

Tahmincioglu, Eve. "Many Teens Face Sexual Harassment on the Job." NBC News, June 7, 2010. http://www.nbcnews.com/id/37320747/ ns/business-careers/t/many-teens-face-sexual-harassment-job.

Yoon-Hendricks, Alexandra. "Berkeley High School Student Sues Alleging School Mishandled Sex Assault Case." *Daily Californian*, November 22, 2016. http://www.dailycal.org/2016/11/22/ berkeley-high-student-sues-alleging-school-mishandled-sex-harassment-case.

Index

A

activism, 88, 90–91
adult harassers, 6, 17, 55
Advocates for Gender Equality club, 90
anxiety, 25, 47, 92
avoiding harassers, 23, 34, 45, 90

B

Berkeley High School, 55–57
bisexual teens, 30
bullying, 10, 23, 35, 37, 38, 84, 86, 91

C

Camp, Anna, 33
campus safety officials, questions for, 58–59
catcalling, 7, 20, 55, 86
Club Fem, 90
Coleman, Angi, 90
compliments, 16
court cases, 7, 53–54, 55, 57, 64

D

date requests, 10, 16–17, 28, 31, 33, 62
death threats, 70, 86
depression, 25, 45
drug abuse, 46, 48

E

emotional support, 50–51, 52
evidence, 35, 55, 64

F

Facebook, 60, 64, 72
flirting, 14–17, 23
friend, being a, 91–94
friend requests, 72

G

gay men and women, 24, 30
Gjoni, Eron, 69–70
Grande, Ariana, 78, 80

H

harassment, myths about, 23–24, 37–39

HeartMob, 86–87
helping victims, 78, 80,
    82–88, 90–94
Hill, Anita, 12–14
Hollywood, 31, 33

I

India, 49–50
Instagram, 20, 64, 71

J

journal writing, 35–36,
    51, 55

L

LastPass, 74
legal action, 35, 53–57
location settings, 76–77

M

mental health, 23, 43,
    50, 70, 77

N

New York City Alliance
    Against Sexual
    Assault, 25, 27
nudes/naked photo-
    graphs, 11, 15, 22,

38, 39, 72

O

objectification, 80
online harassment, 11,
    20, 22, 40, 57, 62,
    64–66, 67, 69–70,
    72, 86–87
online protection,
    71–74, 76–77
online sharing, 64–66
online videos, 35, 39, 66

P

passwords, 73–74, 76
physical contact,
    inappropriate/
    unwanted 11,
    19–20, 39
physical health, 23, 43,
    70, 77
pornography, 11, 20
post-traumatic stress
    disorder (PTSD),
    45–46
pressure, from boy-
    friends, 28
privacy settings, 71–72
Project Girls With Guts,

88, 90

Q

R

Quinn, Zoë, 69–70

rape, 11, 70, 86
relationship status, 66
religious spaces, harassment in, 19–20
remote wiping system, 77

S

school policies, 58
schools, harassment in, 19, 27, 30, 34, 54–57, 76, 86, 88, 90–91
self blame, 11, 43, 51, 92
selfies, 64–65, 67
sexual assault, 11, 27, 53, 88, 90
sexual gestures, 10
sexual graffiti, 11
sexual harassment
  definition, 8, 10
  effects of, 43, 45–46, 48
  examples of, 10–11
  how to help, 78, 80,

82–88, 90–94
  how to tell harassers to stop, 34–35, 37, 62, 82, 86
  percentage of people being sexually harassed, 7, 19, 24, 25, 27–28, 30, 40, 46
  steps to take as a victim, 34–37, 48, 50–51, 53–57
  underreporting of, 39–40, 42
sexual harassment quiz, 37–39
sexual messages/texts, 16, 20, 35, 60, 62, 64, 72
sexual overtones, 10
sexual predators, 20, 66, 72
Sherwood High School, 90
sleep problems, 46, 48
slut shaming, 22
smartphones, 64–71
social media, harassment on, 20, 22
social media abuse, 40,

42
social media blocks, 62, 67, 70
speaking out, 10, 17, 33, 36–37, 42, 82–83, 86
Speak Up—Raising Awareness of Sexual Assault, 90
spreading rumors, 11
Stop Street Harassment, 7
street harassment, 7, 20, 55, 86
suicide, 46, 49–50
support groups, 51

T

therapists and counselors, 45, 53
Thomas, Clarence, 12–14, 35
toxic masculinity, 80, 83–84
trusted adults, confiding in, 35, 36, 53, 69, 86
Tualatin High School, 88, 90
Twitter, 20, 64, 70, 90

U

University of Illinois at Urbana-Champaign, 19
US Senate, 12, 14
US Supreme Court, 12, 14

V

victim blaming, 24
victim profiles, 25, 27–28, 30–31
victims
  blamelessness, 10
  burden of proof, 8
video game developers, 69–70

W

witnesses, 10, 30, 50, 55
workplace harassment, 20, 33

About the Author

IV Thurston is a public relations professional living in Buffalo, New York. Politically active, he has also published widely in newspapers and journals and is an accomplished poet.

Photo Credits

Cover Lisa S./Shutterstock.com; pp. 4–5 © iStockphoto.com/ Art Wager; p. 9 Frizzantine/iStock/Thinkstock; pp. 12–13 Bettmann/Getty Images; p. 15 julief514/iStock/Thinkstock; p. 18 Comstock/Stockbyte/Thinkstock; p. 21 mabe123/iStock/ Thinkstock; pp. 26–27 StphaneLemire/iStock/Thinkstock; pp. 28–29 monkeybusinessimages/iStock/Thinkstock; p. 32 Stefanie Keenan/Getty Images; p. 36 lolostock/iStock/Thinkstock; p. 41 Highwaystarz-Photography/iStock/Thinkstock; pp. 44–45 Tuned_In/iStock/Thinkstock; pp. 47, 54 BrianAJackson/ iStock/Thinkstock; p. 52 Wavebreakmedia Ltd/Thinkstock; p. 61 Astarot/iStock/Thinkstock; pp. 62–63 nandyphotos/iStock/ Thinkstock; p. 65 oneinchpunch/iStock/Thinkstock; p. 68 franviser/Shutterstock.com; p. 75 dolphfyn/iStock/Thinkstock; p. 79 Tinseltown/Shutterstock.com; p. 81 © iStockphoto.com/ KatarzynaBialasiewicz; p. 85 DAJ/Thinkstock; pp. 88–89 JackF/ iStock/Thinkstock; pp. 92–93 Galina Barskaya/Shutterstock.com; cover and interior pages background © iStockphoto.com/Sergei Dubrovski.

Design & Layout: Nicole Russo-Duca; Editor & Photo Research: Heather Moore Niver